The New
Revolutionary War

The New Revolutionary War

An American Firefighter's Dream to Help Save Humanity

John G. Curry

The New Revolutionary War: An American Firefighter's Dream to Help Save Humanity

Published by Iceni Books™
2030 E Speedway Blvd. Suite 106, Tucson AZ 85719.
www.icenibooks.com

Publisher's Cataloging-in-Publication
(Provided by Quality Books, Inc.)

Curry, John G.
    The new revolutionary war : an American firefighter's dream to help save humanity / John G. Curry.
    p. cm.
    LCCN 2005921366
    ISBN 1-58736-451-4

    1. United States--Social conditions--1980- 2. Social change--United States. 3. Cooperation--United States. 4. Social problems--United States.   I. Title.

HN59.2.C877 2005   303.4
                           QBI05-200032

rev202201

Cover illustration designed by
John G. Curry

Illustrated by
Frederick "Hasani" Mabron
Chicago, Illinois

TABLE OF CONTENTS

John G. Curry

PREFACE

I am John G. Curry. Once I was honored to protect the President of the United States when he visited Chicago. This former President said in a speech not long ago, "Americans long to be united." Well, I have an idea that could be used to do just that—unite the people of America. I am honored to present this idea to the American people and to the World. Thank you for this opportunity.

As a Chicago firefighter I have realized my dream of working with an incredible team of men and women to accomplish an honorable mission: to protect life and property. Although I can admit that I am not the greatest firefighter who ever lived, my best effort will be available when the alarm bell rings. The realization that you are part of a team of other individuals with the same honorable goal helps you to understand that it is not necessary for anyone to be greater than anyone else. If everyone is prepared to do their best, the team will have the best chance to succeed in their mission, and all will have satisfaction.

This job of being a firefighter is a way of life that works for me. It has added to my ability to serve as a role model for my two children and future generations of yours. I've had the honor of working with our Public

Education section, speaking to children and adults about fire safety and emergency preparedness—knowledge that might one day save their lives. I worked for years in our Fire Prevention Bureau, believing that prevention is the best way to fight a fire or negate an emergency. This was when my path crossed with that of President Clinton in 1999. Now I work in our Operations Bureau, formerly Fire Suppression and Rescue—the one you call when education and prevention efforts have failed.

I have shared this information about myself with you to begin a comparison to our human condition that can be improved if we unite as a team. That which makes my job as a firefighter a necessary part of our community also necessitates our union. Lives and property are at stake. We must unite to improve the quality of life for all. This quality of life may include the ownership of property by individual choice. But why should you and I care about the quality of life of others? The answer is simple. We are all dependent upon each other within the community—our team, whether we like it or not. As long as anyone is socially or economically disadvantaged, we are all socially and economically disadvantaged.

So in my comparison of our human condition with the honorable career of being a firefighter, we are now at the operations (or fire suppression and rescue) stage. By this I mean that the people within our community have been poorly educated and prepared to deal with the current emergency situation. Efforts to "prevent" the emergency situation from getting out of control have failed. Now who can be called to mitigate this situation for the people whose lives and property are jeopardized? We have failed to maintain the team. Perhaps it never existed. We have failed to recognize that we are all part of the team and must be available to do our best because the alarm bell has already rung.

The emergency situation that I am referring to is the deterioration of our society. The walls of our residence are burning and collapsing around us and many are asleep. We must all wake up like firefighters in the night, understand the emergency, and then respond. That is the purpose of this book—to help facilitate the understanding of the emergency within our society and to encourage action by sharing an idea that is powerful enough to keep our walls from collapsing and get the fire under control. Fire should always be controlled...used to cook our food, to heat our bodies, and for other constructive purposes. My idea can restore this control. The Idea is also powerful enough to build us a new house because now this one is severely damaged. It is an idea that makes it possible for so many people to unite and become honorable.

Enough about me, choice of professions, and that comparison! Let's address the problem of our society. For thousands of years the human race has made the mistake of letting a few people control the many. These few are almost always corrupted by this power, resulting in the abuse of the many. Our society is no different. We all complain about the abuses we endure and the problems we share, but have yet to solve the problem. With all the people of the United States of America exercising their freedom of speech at the same time, only noise is produced, not solutions. The only way to begin solving our problems is by exercising our human and constitutional right to peaceably assemble. We must unite and establish some order in our communications but freely circulate knowledge and ideas. We must unite in a way that is effective against the few who control our society. We must work together to solve our problems. We may then be an example to the World and a catalyst for world peace.

I hope you will allow me to share these possibilities with you all, by your reading of this book and by encouraging all your family, friends, coworkers, and acquaintances to read it also. Please continue....

INTRODUCTION

In the firehouse, I spent much of my free time thinking of ways to solve my problems. Like many Americans, I had selfishly given up on solving our shared problems, after years of retreat from what seemed to be an undefeatable enemy, an enemy that scattered our armies and confounded our socioeconomic condition. One day, over two years ago, I came up with an idea that I felt was the answer to all my problems. Well it was not. But it led to a discovery of The Idea that we can use to put us all back on the track of working together to solve the problems we share. It can be used to do much more than solve our problems; it can be a means of achieving world peace. All this can be accomplished in a relatively short period of time. I estimate it will take one to three years for Americans to be united, if they truly "long to be," as President Clinton asserted. Then it will require at least three to ten years of working together to significantly improve our conditions in America. We will then be in a better position and have the understanding necessary to participate in negotiating world peace. Hopefully, the peoples of the World "long to be united" also. I hope that the international community will also read this book and simultaneously work on their parts of our planetary community so that we may all come together more efficiently.

An idea of such potential and such value to the American people and the World cannot be expressed in a few sentences. I'm sorry about that. I am also faced with the task of presenting this possibility to more than two hundred million American adults and the billions of adults around the World. Each of these adults has different requirements of acceptance. And young adults and children also need to be prepared to join our effort. I am not a skilled writer or salesman. And I am not highly educated. For all these reasons, I will require a great deal of patience, understanding, and help from each of you.

I am sorry that from this point on I will address most of my attention to the American condition, but Americans have certain rights guaranteed by law that facilitate my idea. I am ignorant of the laws and languages of the other countries, so I cannot apply my idea in all countries. However, one of the main concepts is applicable: the many must control themselves or they will be abused.

The *right of the people peaceably to assemble*, not freedom of speech, in my opinion is the most powerful of all the rights identified in the United States Constitution. If we could truly unite and respect each other as individuals with rights to, among others, "Life, Liberty, and the Pursuit of Happiness" (as stated in the Declaration of Independence), we could solve all the problems we share. Then, America could be great. I believe there is a way of actually uniting the people of the United States of America into a force so strong it could change any aspect of our dysfunctional socioeconomic condition. I believe that once united to accomplish the goal of improving these conditions, Americans will form bonds of mutual respect—as soldiers do. This is a war worth fighting. I believe "The Idea" is the appropriate weapon to use.

It is said that peace cannot be obtained through war. I believe the only exception to the rule is a war against the enemies that have plagued the communities of mankind since the dawn of time. These enemies of the people will be identified within this work, a basic strategy for their defeat will be provided, and a powerful weapon will be drafted. Once the American people unite against our common foes in The New Revolutionary War, we can develop respect for each other and all of our lives will improve.

In expressing The Idea that has led me to believe these possibilities, I will follow the order of my thoughts on how to conduct a war against the enemies of our community.

CHAPTER 1

The Problems
(The Provocation)

The need for change is apparent. There are so many problems and concerns that they cannot all be listed here. But as a person with a firefighter mentality, I prepare myself with the knowledge and understanding of many different problems but train with the team to provide solutions. Here is a short list of problems that we can address in our training:

The current war America wages seems to offer fewer benefits than casualties.

We have been and are victims of terrorists (whatever that means). I define terrorist as another selfish person.

We are embarrassed internationally.

Weapons of mass destruction: Did you know that we have over ten thousand? No one in his or her right mind would ever use one in this confined space—Earth. An estimated seventy-five thousand people were killed in Hiroshima and another forty thousand killed in Nagasaki, with hundreds of thousands in both cities who had to live with their injuries. That's not quite like being flatulent in an elevator. It's not funny.

Social Security is always threatened.

The stock market exists and shouldn't. That's just my opinion…and another book.

Real estate prices are going up at such a dispro-portional rate to income levels that the working class eventually will not be able to afford a home or apartment.

There are poor people. I hope this statement doesn't offend anyone. No one has to accept his or her con-dition without trying to improve it. This statement just indicates that there are different class distinc-tions within our society and that it may be unfair.

Wealthy individuals and/or corporations seem to control the government and the economy.

Crime and perversion seem to be acceptable now. Some may take offense to the word perversion. It is not my intention to offend anyone, so I will briefly offer this explanation of my statement: Among consenting adults in a private setting, I would not classify much as perversion. But when an adult or a child past the age of reason engages in some acts with one that is incapable of making a reasonable decision to consent or is forced to participate in the act, there is perversion.

Education is inadequate and/or unaffordable.

Some children are neglected and abused.

Healthcare is expensive and is controlled by the wealthy people of the insurance and pharmaceutical companies or by wealthy people of totally unrelated industries.

Doctors are so threatened by opportunists and their lawsuits that they are defecting.

The environment is being neglected and abused.

Human rights are being violated.

The misuse of religion by individuals damages our society.

The cold war era, with its brainwashing of Americans against communism, has stigmatized the word community so much that anyone attempting to unite the people of America is accused of being communist. Anyone who understands root words would expect the definitions to be similar.

Justice is manipulated.

The people are dissatisfied.

Drugs and alcohol are overused to escape.

Loan sharking is now legal, and state governments are now the "numbers runners" with their lotteries.

Gambling riverboats and other casinos are full of hopeful hopeless people.

Food is dangerous.

And many more …

Sorry I got carried away. Enough is enough. We need to change!

So what is the cause of all this dysfunction? Who or what should we unite against? I will explain.

CHAPTER 2

The Cause
(The Enemy)

Now that was just a glimpse of our socioeconomic condition. We are definitely dysfunctional. To change this condition we first have to understand it. I don't expect more than 290 million Americans to understand things in the exact same way that I do, or to make the same choice of words that I have. However, I wish to encourage all Americans to ponder these subjects to gain their own understanding, as it will be very important in our efforts to unite. Until I receive responses to my presentation, my analysis is all I have to work with. So, I have concluded that Americans and the people of the World suffer from the same things: thousands of years of selfishness, separation, ignorance, and human nature. America was born out of the capitalistic desires and selfishness of our founders and has festered. This truth is now being taught in some elementary schools.

Our economic system, capitalism, is synonymous with selfishness. Our society is induced by this selfishness to separate the people by any means necessary to perpetuate the capitalistic benefits of a few individuals in the form of money and control. Ignorance is also encouraged to perpetuate the monetary wealth and control of the few. And finally, human nature is at the root of all this selfishness.

So, these are our enemies: selfishness, separation, ignorance, and human nature. These are the enemies of every community. But how can we battle these villains? Let us prepare ourselves for battle.

CHAPTER 3

Preparation for Battle
(The Strategy)

Our enemies have been identified as selfishness, separation, ignorance, and human nature. They are concepts. Concepts have to be fought with other concepts or
ideas. When these concepts manifest themselves in our
society and our economic systems, they need to be fought
with The Idea. So, since they originate within each one of
us, a major battle has to be fought within each one of us.
That is where knowledge and philosophy are helpful. All
Americans are encouraged to increase their knowledge
and develop philosophies that will help them eradicate or
minimize the effects of these enemies within themselves,
so we can unite "peaceably." I will share some of the
philosophies and understanding I will use to combat these
concepts. Then I will explain The Idea. Some Americans
may choose to skip this section, but once again I ask for
your patience. There is one aspect of The Idea that is
revealed within the following philosophies. It somewhat
accommodates those Americans who choose not to battle
our enemies within themselves. They will still be able to
join the effort to battle the economic manifestation of our

enemies using The Idea and may later find peace within our society. Let's stay together.

Humans have only a few basic needs: food, water, shelter, and clothing for protection. Just about everything else is for entertainment purposes (to pass the time away between birth and death): reproduction, sex, companionship, competition, selfishness, love, religion, drugs, crime, helping, trying to save the World from self-destruction, baseball, etc. The human nature that seeks to supply the basic needs is the same or similar in all of us, but some humans choose forms of entertainment that damage our society, which is selfish. The Golden Rule, as some call it, is articulated in almost as many different words as there are individuals. One version is the biblical one: "Do unto others as you would have them do unto you." (My wording may be different from yours.) Another is "to treat people as you would want to be treated." This is a very good rule, but in a society where people abuse themselves, they will abuse others if they follow this rule. I believe all people are free, within reason, to do anything they want as long as it does not interfere with another person's freedoms, rights, or safety. We have to learn to respect each other. We must suppress our own selfish human nature so that we can work together to improve conditions for all Americans.

Ignorance is fought with knowledge. As a firefighter, I was trained to fight a fire by understanding it. Taking away one or more of the components of combustion—heat, oxygen (or an oxidizing agent), fuel, or the self-sustained chemical chain reaction, will put the fire out. You also have to understand the conditions of the fire scene that may become factors. Sun Tzu's ancient strategies in the *Art of War* say basically the same thing——to defeat a powerful enemy you have to know him/her/them and the conditions of the battlefield. All Americans must continue to educate themselves. We have a real war to fight, and all soldiers can contribute their knowledge, strength, and common sense toward the success of the unit. All Americans should be willing to share their knowledge and resources to help in this fight. When we pool all this information, we must analyze it and develop solutions to our problems—together. The methods of understanding of firefighters and Sun Tzu can be applied during the analysis.

Understanding the conditions of the battlefield (or fire scene) is more complicated. The mediums through which the controlling few ration, manipulate, and fabricate information cannot be blindly trusted. Their craft has been perfected for thousands of years and passed down to the new generations of selfish people. It is in their best interest to keep us ignorant. Ignorance is passed down also, but it is passed down to the controlled masses. Even the history that we try to learn from was written by those few who were in control at the time. Sometimes, a few powerful people destroyed all records of the truth and history was written much later than the actual times. Some events never happened but were authenticated. We must carefully examine all information of the past, present, and future, especially the information that comes from those that were, are, or will be in control of our society. We must also resist the distractions that the controlling few tempt us with to accomplish their selfish goals.

Selfishness is a choice, and choices are made for reasons of each individual. Many of these reasons stem from conditioning during psychosexual and psychosocial stages of development. Although I am aware of these approaches to explain why people are the way that they are, I am not licensed to do anything but sell real estate (I am not active) and be a firefighter at the first-responder level. So to fight selfishness, I can only offer suggestions or encourage you to find your own reason to make the choice to join the fight to save America. Consider John Nash's theory of equilibrium in noncooperative games, which, like the theories of Sun Tzu, have been used to strengthen our enemies against us. This is my understanding of this theory: an individual within a group of other individuals all desiring the same or similar objects or outcome will benefit more if he/she does what's best for the group and the individual. Therefore, all Americans desiring life, liberty, and the pursuit of happiness, and other things that this country could facilitate, should do what's best for all Americans, and that will be what's beneficial to them because they are Americans. That is, help fix our shared problems instead of being part of the problem. Another example of this equilibrium theory: I have often heard that the bonds that are created among soldiers during wartime are strong. Or, the bonds of those abused together can also be strong for the same reason—dependency on one another to work together to mitigate the situation so that all will obtain relief. So we should all come together as unselfish people and fight *pro bono publico*, for the good and welfare of the public. And, even if we just come together as we are, realizing our dependency upon each other, we may form the strong bonds that soldiers and abused persons form.

Separation is also a choice. At first I thought if I could solve the mysteries that separate the religious, I would have half this battle won. Well, I finally figured it out, but the answer only won me my freedom from religious limitations to my spirituality. I would love to share this answer with everyone, but those who have never questioned the religions that they were born into or rescued by may be offended or shattered. As I will say over and over again, it is not my intention to offend or harm anyone. I am trying to bring people together for their mutual benefit and offending would not help. I have learned that although we may disagree religiously, I can respect anyone's religious choice and can be happy for him or her if it strengthens them psychologically and morally and if it doesn't damage our community. We must all strive to understand and respect the religious choices of others to unite. We must also gain at least a basic knowledge of psychology and how it affects the choices humans make. That will help in the understanding.

Religion is only one of so many devices that are used to separate human beings. I tried to understand the psychological fallout of slavery, the holocaust, the displacement or slaughter of the Native Americans, discrimination against women, genocide, and many other major human abuses that contribute to the separation of mankind. I tried to learn how fear is exploited to separate and manipulate the masses. All these efforts to understand separation were so that we could come together and not let all our negative feelings interfere with our necessary task. In every abuse of humans by humans and every situation where humans separated from one another, I found selfishness as the cause. Nothing has changed. Selfishness is still encouraging us to separate. We must change our minds.

No one should ever forget the past, but when our future is jeopardized by the past or present, we must choose not to perpetuate the worst of those times. We especially should not abuse those who are not directly responsible for abuses suffered. This only increases the effect of separation, by design of the controlling few. Also, our fear must be conquered individually or with the help of others. The strength in numbers can replace fear with courage. As I said of the other choice, selfishness, which was and is the cause of all separation, I can only offer suggestions or encouragement to minimize separation so we can work together. I find some peace and understanding in the sayings of Jiddu Krishnamurti, who has been quoted as saying, "The symbols, ideas, and beliefs that man has constructed as a fence of security are concepts only, the causes of problems which create a false sense of individuality, dividing one person from another." Within our economy and our society, we are all dependent upon each other, whether we like it or not. We must find a way to respect or tolerate each other and unite. If we unite, the fear will be obliterated by the power of the union. I have found one possible way to unite and acquire this power: The Idea. And I will share it shortly.

There are three more things I would like to share with you before I disclose The Idea. One is a theory I used when I was religious to give me hope for the salvation of the World. My sister said it gives her hope that supplements her religious beliefs. So I will include it in this book for anyone it may comfort. I was born into a Christian family, so I believed as they do. However, I had a big problem accepting the inevitable doom of Revelation. I was taught to believe in God as my father. So, like my earthly father who was a logical, reasonable, compassionate, and loving man, I attributed these traits to God. If my father had told me to clean up my room or he would beat me, I would have cleaned it to avoid the beating. He would not have punished me. So it would stand to reason that a reasonable, loving, logical, compassionate, and merciful God would not punish us as foretold if we made a sincere effort to "clean up our room." Please help me. Let us straighten up this mess.

The second thing I must write of before my idea is revealed is the concept of supply and demand. I will briefly discuss this for those who may not be familiar with its involvement in our economy. And, since the two factors that affect our society are human nature and economics, we must also understand this major part of economics. The concept of supply and demand is a way of predicting the spending habits of consumers. These predictions are used to maximize the profits of major capitalists, by establishing a market value of goods and services. When the supply of a good or service increases and demand remains stable, prices go down to attract more buyers; when demand increases and supply remains stable, prices go up because the buyers compete for the product. This is just a simplified summary of the principles of supply and demand. American consumers should all take the time to read more on this subject to understand the manipulation that takes place in our marketplaces. This will help you understand how it can be counteracted through our unity.

There is another dimension to supply and demand that is the key to minimizing or stopping this manipulation and abuse of consumers. It is a weapon to use in fighting the economic part of our war. If people join together in great numbers and can control supply, they can meet their own demands for a little over cost. No owner of a company pays the full marked-up price for the product he/she makes. Anyone performing a service for himself/herself does it at the cost of the materials. The payment for their work is in the form of the benefits the service provides. If the great number of people who unite choose not to control supply, they can choose to control the suppliers by demanding as one and significantly lowering the price of the good or service. While working together toward this common goal of controlling supply or suppliers, they will develop respect for one another, as soldiers do, and strengthen our society.

In addition to controlling supply and suppliers, and working on our social problems, the union can also have more control of another element of our society that has gotten out of hand—our government. This is the third and last subject that will precede the presentation of The Idea.

As I explained earlier when I wrote of Sun Tzu's *Art of War*, you must understand the conditions of the battlefield in addition to knowing the enemy, which has been identified as selfishness, separation, ignorance, and the part of human nature at the root of selfishness. Our government controls the conditions of the battlefield—American economics. We are supposed to control the government—as we have been led to believe. Some Americans believe this is impossible, while others believe that we are controlling our government by voting. Our responsibility as Americans does not end with the election of our government officials, and it *is* possible to control the government.

Just after the "Life, Liberty ..." bit in the *Declaration of Independence*, it explains:

> That to secure these rights, governments are instituted among men, deriving their just powers from the consent of the governed—that whenever any form of government becomes destructive of these ends, it is the right of the people to alter or to abolish it, and to institute new government, laying its foundation on such principles and organizing its powers in such form, as to them shall seem most likely to effect their safety and happiness.

Change is one of the powers reserved by the American people. I encourage all Americans to empower themselves by uniting to accomplish the original idealistic goals that are sold to us as the American dream. The few are not supposed to control the many. Wealthy individuals and corporations are not supposed to control our government. That is not democracy. Only exercising our right to assemble will give us the ability to control our government together.

This assembly would also be an opportunity to combine our efforts on other problems and issues that we have in common, such as healthcare, education, social security, and crime. It could be a medium to share knowledge, strength, and ideas. It could be a forum to iron out our differences. It would be a big step in the direction of world peace. The benefits would be limitless. Let's do this! Here's how.

CHAPTER 4

The Idea
(The Weapon)

How do Americans unite? To answer this question we must first answer the questions of how and why were we separated. Then reverse the process.

The *Declaration of Independence* created America. Because selfish people created our government, it was designed as it was and is. And, the people were to be kept separated. Americans were united briefly to replace the King with the new selfish rulers, who would separate the people further to maintain control. The colonial people at that time were just led to believe that they had an opportunity to start over and were going to be included this time. That is why they fought the Revolutionary War. The new government was setup in a way that mirrored the way the Virginia colony was governed: the Royal Governor position (the King's flunky who ruled the colony) would now be called President. The House of Burgesses members were citizens of Virginia who were elected lawmakers of the colony. Only white men with property were allowed to vote. They were broken up in 1774 by the Royal Governor and had to meet secretly in a tavern. Later they met with representatives of other colonies as the Continental Congress. This merger would later become our Senate and House of Representatives. And the judges became the judicial branch of our government. So you see everything stayed basically the same, except control was shifted. So who controls our economy, our society, and our government today? Wealthy individuals and their corporations control all three.

To reverse the process of the separation of the American people, we have to become a corporation and a wealthy individual. United in this way, we can participate in controlling our government, our economy, and ultimately our society. Once we get knowledgeable and strong enough, we can remove any other controlling corporations and wealthy individuals by our great numbers of people united. Because these united Americans will have lost their selfishness in The New Revolutionary War, America can begin again and all Americans can pursue their lives, their liberties, and their happiness together as one community. To explain The Idea I need to define several terms using *Merriam-Webster's 11th Collegiate Dictionary* (computer version).

Please, take a moment to examine these definitions:

Corporation

1a: a group of merchants or traders united in a trade guild b: the municipal authorities of a town or city

2: a body formed and authorized by law to act as a single person although constituted by one or more persons and legally endowed with various rights and duties including the capacity of succession

3: an association of employers and employees in a basic industry or of members of a profession organized as an organ of political representation in a corporative state

4: POTBELLY 1

ᏣᏍᏏᎧᏣ

Capitalist

1: a person who has capital especially invested in business; *broadly*: a person of wealth: PLUTOCRAT

2: a person who favors capitalism

ᏣᏍᏏᎧᏣ

Capitalism

An economic system characterized by private or corporate ownership of capital goods, by investments that are determined by private decision, and by prices, production, and the distribution of goods that are determined mainly by competition in a free market

ᏣᏍᏏᎧᏣ

Putting It All Together

The second definition of *corporation* is most important: a body formed and authorized by law to act as a single person, although constituted by one or more persons, and legally endowed with various rights and duties including the capacity of succession.

By uniting in this way, we become a single person in the eyes of the law—a single virtually immortal person with many rights composed of many people—that's power. Then, let's put lots of money in this person's pocket and make him/her wealthy—that's power to operate in a capitalistic economy. Part of the definition of capitalist is a wealthy person. Although this person is wealthy, he-she (I must use this generic name so no one is offended), being composed of many persons that have bonded in war, is not selfish, so he-she does not favor capitalism. These people that compose he-she are not competing with each other. They have united to take control of capitalism (by controlling supply, suppliers, and our demand) and supplant it with a new economic system, to be named later, that is less selfish and promotes better relationships between Americans. To minimize the selfishness of this person we will be creating, he-she must be organized in a very special way—a way in which no other corporation (to my knowledge) has been organized. I need to define a few more terms at this time using the same dictionary.

More Definitions

Democracy

1 a: government by the people; *especially*: rule of the majority b: a government in which the supreme power is vested in the people and exercised by them directly or indirectly through a system of representation usually involving periodically held free elections

2: a political unit that has a democratic government

3: *capitalized*: the principles and policies of the Democratic party in the United States [from emancipation Republicanism to New Deal Democracy — C. M. Roberts]

4: the common people especially when constituting the source of political authority

5: the absence of hereditary or arbitrary class distinctions or privileges

Pure democracy

Democracy in which the power is exercised directly by the people rather than through representatives

Social democracy

1: a political movement advocating a gradual and peaceful transition from capitalism to socialism by democratic means

2: a democratic welfare state that incorporates both capitalist and socialist practices

Tory democracy

A political philosophy advocating preservation of established institutions and traditional principles combined with political democracy and a social and economic program designed to benefit the common man

Taking the best parts of all these definitions, we real-ize the corporation must not be organized as a typical corporation. It must be organized as a democracy, a pure and social democracy. The last definition of democracy, "the absence of hereditary or arbitrary class distinctions or privileges," is very important. Every American who is part of this unity, this corporation, must be equal. How do you accomplish this equality? Easy! Only one share of stock in the corporation is to be issued to each American. No one will have more shares than anyone else. All will own the corporation equally. All will have equal voting rights. All will vote directly, and the majority vote (percentage to be established by vote) will determine the actions of the whole body of the corporation—not a board of directors.

Parts of the Tory democracy definition can be included in our goal of this corporation for this country. We do not want to overthrow the government of this country; we just want it to be fair, respectable, strong, and in the control of the many whom it represents. We definitely want ben-eficial social and economic programs for all Americans. Looking further into the origin of Tory may stigmatize the word, but the definition as it is stated in my dictionary of choice is how it is to be regarded in this work.

Let's Talk Money

Remember when I said let's put lots of money in he-she's pockets? How much is "lots" of money? How much would be effective in today's economy? The following is as this whole book has been—my opinion.

We are not all rich. We are at very different financial levels. What is affordable for some is devastating for others. But as I said, the shares of stock, the ownership, and the voting rights in the corporation must be equal. Everyone knows that if you collect one dollar from one

million people you will have one million dollars. There
are more than 290 million Americans in the United States.
Approximately two hundred million are adults. I project
only a small percentage of these adults will join this effort
initially—hopefully at least 10 percent. I will make calcu-
lations based on that figure. So, if you collect one dollar
from twenty million people, he-she would have $20 mil-
lion in his-her pocket. In my opinion, that's not enough.
Each share in this unity needs to cost one hundred dollars,
thus constituting $2 billion of start-up capital for the cor-
poration. Then he-she will be strong.

This money does not need to be carried around in his-
her pocket, and for the most part does not need to be spent.
It's leverage. But where is the safest place to hold it? I feel
the safest place to hold most of it is in the U.S. Treasury.
That way it is guaranteed by the stability of the U.S. government that we intend to preserve and strengthen, and
it will earn more interest than any U.S. bank is offering
and be at no risk of loss, as other investments may have.
In addition to our efforts to strengthen the government
through our control, our deposit of so much money, with
more to come, will also strengthen our country.

Now that we know where to keep it, let's get back to
collecting it. I think most Americans waste much more
than one hundred dollars during the year and can extract it
from these entertainment funds. However, there are some
Americans who honestly can't afford to part with one hundred dollars at one time. Perhaps they won't be able to part
with it at all. Those who can come up with it over time will
be able to pay over time (please start saving now). Those
who really can't come up with it at all (please be honest),
must be helped by those who can afford more. Hopefully
their friends, family, churches, etc. will give them a loan
or gift of this one-time expense. If not, the kindness of
strangers will help increase our numbers by including

these significant individuals. All Americans are important in this effort. Hopefully those who don't join initially will see us succeed in our goals and join later. The door will always be open.

Speaking of the door being open, the shares of stock, which give each person equal ownership and equal rights in the corporation, should not be sold on the open market. Trading of this stock should not be allowed. It should not be offered publicly. These measures will protect the corporation from the many controls our government, which is controlled by corporations and wealthy people, has in place to keep people separated. So, the door may be open for new people to enter, but should not encourage people to leave. Perhaps a buy-back policy can be established later.

So how can the stock be offered privately? That is simple. It will be offered the same way information is spread—through word of mouth between people who are connected to each other, such as friends, family, coworkers, members of religious congregations, neighbors, etc. We are all connected in this way, and once the spread of information gets started, all will be exposed quickly. Building upon these existing personal bonds will also strengthen our corporation by adding trust to the union. While we are earning each other's trust, we can rely on the trust that has already been established in our personal lives. The number of people you trust who join you in this effort diminishes the fear of trusting new people, proportionally. You can protect each other and discuss old and new concepts, such as this one I propose, as you normally would—with someone you trust. When you go somewhere new or try something you have never tried before, doesn't it help to have someone you trust with you?

Consider this example: One person (me) had an idea that was worth sharing, and I shared it with two people with whom I had a strong relationship (two of my sisters), and then each one of my sisters shared it with one of her friends at work and with a friend from her past, and then

week	People exposed each week	Total number of people exposed	Total capital
1	1		$100
2	2	3	$300
3	4	7	$700
4	8	15	$1,500
5	16	31	$3,100
6	32	63	$6,300
7	64	127	$12,700
8	128	255	$25,500
9	256	511	$51,100
10	512	1023	$102,300
11	1024	2047	$204,700
12	2048	4095	$409,500
13	4096	8191	$819,100
14	8192	16383	$1,638,300
15	16384	32767	$3,276,700
16	32768	65535	$6,553500
17	65536	131071	$13,107,100
18	131072	262143	$26,214,300
19	262144	524287	$52,428,700
20	524288	1048575	$104,857,500
21	1048576	2097151	$209,715,100
22	2097152	4194303	$419,430,300
23	4194304	8388607	$838,860,700
24	8388608	16777215	$1,677,721,500
25	16777216	33554431	$3,355,443,100
26	33554432	67108863	$6,710,886,300
27	67108864	134217727	$13,421,772,700

those people each shared it with their family and friends (at least two people for this example), and so on. The chart on the previous page indicates how fast the information would spread. It also indicates how much money would be raised if one hundred dollars was collected from each of these persons. Also indicated is how many weeks it would take to spread this information if each new group of people exposed only took one week to share this information with their two friends, family members, or associates.

So in less than one year, more than half the adult population of the United States could be exposed to this great idea, and if they all joined this effort, more than $13 billion of start-up capital could be amassed. This example only takes into account every person exposing two more people. I have five sisters and a brother, many coworkers, some friends, neighbors, etc., and each of these people is not limited to sharing this idea with two people, and so on. Some people I've met belong to clubs, fraternities, and other organizations of hundreds of people who can all be exposed at one time. Exposure to groups would greatly reduce the amount of time it would take to share this information.

Each time another person is added to the people who are exposed to this idea through you is an opportunity for you and other shareholders to network with this person. We all have knowledge of different things from our life experiences that can be shared. This new person is someone who is trusted by someone who will be somehow related to you. So even if you don't know this person, or you know them but don't care for this new person, they are peaceably connected to someone you know. So you are indirectly connected to their contributions to our effort and they are to yours. Finally, our corporation will connect all these streams of relationships. So as long as one person within one of these streams is actively participating in the activity of the corporation, all should be informed by someone they trust.

On the subject of how people can be remotely connected to each other, here's a perfect illustration. I began this book the same way I started my Internet presentation of my idea—with my connection to former President Clinton. This was an attempt to get your attention and to allow you to take me seriously. But here, I'm only listing that night as one of three ways that I am connected to Bill. I use his first name because my relatives provide me with my other two connections. One relative had a relationship with him as a child and another still has a relationship with him now. The relative that knows him now and I have recently begun our relationship. But through new connections, we may gain access to knowledge and experiences that we never dreamed of having. One day I may share a conversation with this man who has experienced being President of the United States of America. Back to The Idea, the spread of information and the chart....

Some people might look at the chart or hear the process and be quick to label this spread of information and call to arms a pyramid scheme. These people don't fully understand what a pyramid scheme is. So that no one is excluded, I will have to briefly explain pyramid schemes and how they are not applicable in this case:

The Illinois Compiled Statutes has the following definition:

(815 ILCS 505/1)
Sec. 1.
(g) The term "pyramid sales scheme" includes any plan or operation whereby a person in exchange for money or other thing of value acquires the opportunity to receive a benefit or thing of value,

which is primarily based upon the inducement of additional persons, by himself or others, regardless of number, to participate in the same plan or operation and is not primarily contingent on the volume or quantity of goods, services, or other property sold or distributed or to be sold or distributed to persons for purposes of resale to consumers. For purposes of this subsection, "money or other thing of value" shall not include payments made for sales demonstration equipment and materials furnished on a nonprofit basis for use in making sales and not for resale.

In forming this corporation, no one is paid to induce their family, friends, coworkers, and special acquaintances to join. They are only obligated to share the information with people they care about because it is in the best interest of the person to be exposed. If they choose not to share this information or opportunity with anyone, they will not be excluded in any way from any benefits of belonging to the united Americans. This is only a way of sharing information. If a cure for cancer was found, the information would spread this same way and there would be no accusations of a pyramid scheme. When someone is organizing a march against criminal activity, they invite their friends and family to join them. They also ask these people to bring in as many other people as they can to make the march more effective. This is not considered a pyramid. In this corporation, there is only one level because all persons have equal ownership. That is not true of pyramids. Let's move on.

The Body of the Corporation

Since we are creating a person and have little or no guidance in doing so, we would be wise to find a rather successful model—the human body—to imitate. The different and necessary systems the corporation will need to function efficiently can be compared to the systems and organs of our bodies. The first and probably most important area to be set up should be communication.

Communication between the shareholders is the brains of this person we create. And like the electrical impulses that are involved in our decision making, the people that comprise this person will make decisions for this person through communication of information and voting. This person will be educated through the education of his-her shareholders. This brain will constantly process the information of problems and other issues and develop solutions.

The pathway through which the different parts of the body communicate with the brain will be compared with the central nervous system (CNS). If we examine the functions and relationships of the parts of the CNS (brain, medulla oblongata, and spinal cord) and how signals are communicated with body parts, we will probably gain more insight into how to organize our communication.

The circulatory system will carry vital nutrients (money, benefits, knowledge, etc.) throughout the body. When a need is communicated through the central nervous system, resources will be allocated through this system.

The respiratory system will be the means of bringing in the knowledge we need and infusing it into the circulatory system.

Also, the digestive system can be compared to some aspect of the corporation. The money can enter the body through this system. Once it is converted into usable vitamins, minerals, and other necessary nutrients, the body will share the converted material with the other parts of the body through absorption through the intestinal walls. If we use this resource efficiently, there will be little waste at the end of the processing.

The skeletal system may turn out to be the corporate structure itself. The officers of the corporation (president, vice president, secretary, etc.) can be part of this system. They will act as directed by the shareholders through a system of muscles, ligaments, and tendons to perform administrative functions only.

The arms and legs of this person are many. They will number as high as the number of persons who comprise this person, and will be capable of doing much work.

We also need to develop a system of fighting disease within the body. An immune system will combat selfishness within the corporation.

How about reproduction? It may become necessary to create subsidiary corporations to help us obtain our goals.

Of course these are just philosophical comparisons to serve as a guide in organizing this corporation. They were helpful in my visualization of the concept of creating this champion of the people.

Speaking of champions of the people, let's talk about leaders. A leader of the past was a man, woman, or child who had their own agendas, limitations, and flaws. In the past, there have been many visionaries who have tried to change the World for the better. Some have tried to change it for the worse, but let's not give them validation. The positive leaders made their contributions to their societies, managed to get themselves into the history books, and then died or were killed. The people who followed them dissipated. Some tried to continue the movements, but they were not as effective as these visionaries. These are all reasons why we should create our own leader. This person we create when we unite as a corporation can serve as our leader. There are only two things that can kill this leader and scatter the members of this community. The first is if it is by choice of the members to abandon the cause. Once united, that is unlikely. Remember "Americans long to be united." Second is an act of law. Any such act would violate one of the first rights guaranteed to us in the First Amendment of the Constitution of the United States—our right to peaceably assemble. So this new kind of leader is immortal. His-her agenda is established by vote—a true leader of a democratic nation. He-she has few limitations and is only flawed by our individual selfishness, which we are committed to working on. He-she is perfect. If you have gotten this far in reading this work, you have made an unselfish achievement—thank you.

Back on the subject of selfishness, there are more precautions that I recommend we take to protect the trust that would be developed within the corporation. They include preventing individuals from stealing from and doing other things that may embarrass the union. We can't allow corporate scandals to separate us after we worked so hard to come together. Within the bylaws there must be provisions for the shareholders to view information of all transfers and disbursements of money and all actions taken in the name of the corporation. All actions should be authorized in writing after resolutions of the shareholders have been documented. The shareholders must actively participate in the decision-making processes and the monitoring of corporate actions. All Americans should continue to educate themselves in any and all subjects that will make our union stronger. Let's explore some possible applications of the power of our unity.

CHAPTER 5

Power of Unity
(The Battles)

Caution: Because I am very radical, I'm reluctant to offer my opinions on how to use the power of the corporation. I am not a formally educated economist and can't accurately project the effects of any action that we may choose to take on any issue. But, for the purpose of illustrating the potential of the force we can create when we unite, I will share some of these radical opinions. They should not be a means of alienating anyone from the union of Americans. I feel that out of millions of people, we should have many experts who will share their knowledge and their abilities by making presentations to the other members and they will help us to make informed decisions on all the issues of concern. Together we should decide how to solve our problems and not look to any traditional leader to solve our problems for us. I am not trying to be the leader of this group of people who assemble to form a corporation. I would be easily discredited as such. However, I am prepared to do much more than my share of the work. The person we create is our leader and is controlled by the many people who share equally in him-her.

We should cautiously make educated decisions and then act to change our socioeconomic condition. Please do not let these examples negatively affect any opinions you may have formed. We have come so far.

My Opinions

I'll start with the healthcare problem. Insurance companies and pharmaceutical companies control healthcare. The owners of hospitals, suppliers of equipment, and other capitalists also affect it. Our corporation or one of its children can become an insurance company and insure its shareholders. We would have more than $2 billion of capital to back this venture. Once created, the premiums would support this subsidiary. The loss of premiums will weaken the control the existing insurance companies have on the healthcare industry. We can also build our own labs and develop (research included) our own pharmaceuticals that we can produce in our own factories. We can distribute these pharmaceuticals to our members and to other potential members at slightly-above costs—we can own the patents so we can set fair prices. This will weaken the control of pharmaceutical companies. We can also use the newfound control of our government to change laws that allow these companies to control healthcare and control our politicians. We can remove politicians who are not accountable to the people. We can own our hospitals. We can manufacture our equipment and supplies. We can educate many doctors (increasing supply also lowers the cost of their services) and obligate them to work for a period of time to pay for that education. We can own the universities and schools on all levels and provide quality education to all for much less than we pay selfish capitalists.

There is so much we can do if we are united and want to change. The American people are preoccupied with entertainment. If this person we create can supply a major part of our entertainment desires, the monies we spend on entertainment can also be applied toward healthcare, education, housing, food, water, social security, and much more. More Americans would have the opportunities to share their talents for less pay, but the benefits to all would be tremendous.

An extreme example: What if we televised high school games of football, baseball, hockey, basketball, etc., and the students got the pleasure of being on TV. They need not be paid salaries; they were going to play anyway. They can be fed. Uniforms and equipment to protect them and healthcare can be provided for them. Their families and friends get to watch them and have great conversations. People can support the high schools that they graduated from. The students will also get exposure to professional teams that we can eventually own, and we direct profits to our common goals. Paraphernalia can be sold to support these teams. The revenues collected from the games and any paraphernalia that might be sold, could build schools, pay teachers, buy books and school supplies for the students, support national healthcare and retirement programs, and more. This was just an extreme example of one possibility. It is not a recommendation.

We could own media companies, Internet service providers, wireless phone companies, regular wired phone companies, music and movie companies, grocery stores, construction companies—everything. The cost of the goods and services could and would be much less, and revenues from these companies could be used for all of our benefit—not just for the benefit of the few. This is not communism; this is control of capitalism so the many will benefit more. We can own banks or savings and loan companies. We can control, or abandon, the stock market.

We can restore the whole purpose of mass production—to produce more goods for less money so that the many can benefit from lower prices, increased availability, and jobs. In our capitalistic economy, mass-producing companies charge the maximum amount of money people will pay for goods, according to supply and demand, and frequently lay off workers, both of which defeat the purpose. They use this money to pay the officers and board members too much money, while the workers struggle to support themselves and their families. Sometimes they lay off many of the employees, decreasing their ability to provide the goods that they originally set out to produce for the many. Owning our supplying companies will control availability of products, prices, jobs, and salaries, and control the longevity and retirement potential of our jobs. The owners of companies take care of themselves and their families. We would all be the owner.

I believe that revenues from supplying our own entertainment and from supplying all of our other needs can be shared and applied to our economy, to ease the burdens of all Americans. Then, we can spend more time working on our social problems. These revenues can also support all these social efforts. But first we have to unite in a way to take control of our economics and our society—as a wealthy democratic corporation.

My opinions on governmental applications of power are many, but I'll just include one in this short book. One of the biggest mistakes the American people make is allowing our elected officials to do anything they want. They are elected to do what the people want. But, there is no system set up to find out what the people want. If we, the people, are united, we will be able to express what we want. Why should we allow a few hundred people, or one, to commit more than 293 million people to war without asking us? Of course our armies should be deployed immediately to protect us on United States land. But, before we extend the fight to other countries we should be consulted. We should not have to protest after war is declared. Our sons and daughters are the ones committed to these wars. We must unite!

There are many ways of applying the power of the united American people. I have only shared a few of my thoughts on this. In addition to the applications on existing problems and issues, it would also be advantageous to be united to address future concerns. We can also consider charitable activities and must always consider world peace a possibility.

CHAPTER 6

Conclusion
(Peace)

Peace is undoubtedly more difficult than war. Mankind has proven this for thousands of years by our inability to cooperate our communities into one. There had to be a class system, even among nations. For millennia the nations have jockeyed for position in this class system. This is a result of the selfishness that drives us to contend with each other as individuals and the separation and ignorance that allows a few to commit many to international dysfunction. Throughout history you will find evidence to convict our ancestors and us for our part in perpetuating this madness. It is time, I hope, for us to begin a new trend in history. It is time to move our interpersonal and international relationships toward peace and not toward contention and war.

Conveying peace is also difficult. But I have to believe that peace and its conveyance are not impossible. During a brief moment in June of 2004 I experienced peace. If sharing this peace had been as simple as sharing a hug I may have been able to maintain the level of peace that was achieved. Then the spread of this peace would have only been limited by the time it would take to pass along a hug to six to ten billion people. It was not that simple. I was faced with the challenge of converting peace into words and presenting these words to people who didn't want to hear or listen to me. There was great loss in the conversion, but I am doing my best to express the possibility of peace.

My peace of last June came from the understanding of human nature that my son, now five years old, helped me achieve. For most of my forty years in this wilderness I have tried to understand mankind. But our nature was never as clear as he explained through his innocent actions. It was a day like many others that we were together. We were in the kitchen and he had just eaten his dinner. I was cleaning up and he was playing with the magnets on the refrigerator. After going to the table to get the last of the dishes I had to wash, I turned to find the refrigerator severely abused. He had taken the magnets and scraped the back matter all over the refrigerator doors. This magnet residue was alarming, but I have always tried to scale down my aggressions toward my children—I love them. So I asked him sternly, "What are you doing?" as I removed the magnets from his hand. He did not answer. He had this blank look on his face. So I asked him a second question, "Why did you do that?" Again he did not answer. He did not know why he chose to entertain himself in that way. He never considered that his actions would result in loss to himself or others. As he began to cry, I had to decide how to punish him for his actions and how to clean the refrigerator before his mother got home—so that he would not have to be punished three times. Why three times? Remember, he began to cry, so he was punishing himself because he knew he had disappointed his Daddy. I sent him up to his room while I decided.

As I went to get a bucket of soapy water and a rag, I thought about him and his crime. I realized it was not a crime at all and remembered that I love him. Somehow, perhaps by accident, he had discovered that the magnet material would come off the back of the magnets onto the refrigerator. It became entertaining to him and he got carried away. During the process of fulfilling my responsibility of cleaning up after dinner, I was negligent. Although we were in the same room, I did not watch him closely enough to prevent him from costing us this time away from each other. Was it as much my fault as his? No! There was no fault at all. He was doing what was natural to him, entertaining himself, and I was doing what needed to be done. So I decided that his punishment would only be to watch me clean up his mess so that he would know that his actions might inconvenience others, especially those he loves. Cleaning the refrigerator was not as hard as I imagined. After cleaning it, we shared a hug and I had understanding and peace.

This story may mean nothing to you, but it did provide me with the understanding I required. It is the nature of humans to entertain themselves, but it is selfish to do this at the expense of others. Selfishness will always result in separation and ignorance. These simple truths that I have accepted are the basis of the peace that will sustain me for the duration of my life. But, I'm almost sure they will not be enough for all of you, so I will continue my effort to explain peace.

Again, let us apply the methods of firefighters and philosophers to our understanding of peace. For common reference, I will state the definitions found in my dictionary (same).

Peace

1: a state of tranquillity or quiet: *as* a: freedom from civil disturbance b: a state of security or order within a community provided for by law or custom [a breach of the peace]

2: freedom from disquieting or oppressive thoughts or emotions

3: harmony in personal relations

4 a: a state or period of mutual concord between governments b: a pact or agreement to end hostilities between those who have been at war or in a state of enmity

5: — used interjectionally to ask for silence or calm or as a greeting or farewell
–at peace: in a state of concord or tranquillity

The peace of the second and third definitions is the peace that I claim for myself. You can choose to claim this peace through the understanding of yourself and of others. I have tried to simplify this process of obtaining this peace, but it is a process that involves much introspection and observance. The other definitions of peace can only be achieved through cooperative effort.

For a community to have security and order and to be free from civil disturbance and to have all this provided by law or custom, we must all have the peace that comes from the suppression of selfishness. Then, as unselfish people, we must re-examine our laws and customs and reform them. We must have control of our society to reform customs, our government to reform our laws, and we must control our economics to control our society and our government. For there to be a lasting period of mutual concord between governments or lasting pacts or agreements to end hostilities between those who have been at war or are in states of enmity, the many, who governments are instituted to provide for, must be in control of their governments and must not be selfish.

The Idea that I have tried to express in this book could effectively facilitate the shift in control, peacefully. But the suppression of selfishness has to be done voluntarily on an individual basis. The last definition of peace re-emphasizes this point. I must ask you for your participation in creating this world peace that I propose. I cannot demand it. I humbly ask you all for your help in pouring the foundation for a new peaceful community.

This foundation that I spoke of is for the new house that was alluded to in the preface. The house is metaphorically the center of each individual's economic stability, safety, and happiness. Our new house must have a new economic system that can only come about by taking control of the existing selfish system, capitalism, and agreeing to replace it with one that is beneficial to all. Peace, love, respect, cooperation, and other positives that are realized through suppression of selfish human nature turn houses into homes. All the positive aspects of interpersonal relationships are needed to correct our dysfunctional society to make our new house a home suitable for future generations of human beings.

These future generations will all start out as children, so we must pay special attention during their psychosexual and psychosocial stages of development. The special attention that we have to pay is to ourselves. You see, these children already have peace. It is our responsibility not to disturb it. Those of us who chose or will choose to reproduce have this great responsibility, as do those who are unable or choose not to reproduce. So I repeat: It is our responsibility not to disturb the peace of our children. We must protect them from the selfishness that simmers or boils within all of us, and the damage that it has caused.

This will be the hardest but most important part of our effort toward American and world peace. We can win the economic and political war, if we unite with suppressed selfishness. I have shown you how simple this would be. Uniting in this way will lead to a level of peace that has not been realized in the documented history of mankind. But to create lasting peace, we must change the mold that produces selfish human beings, so that selfishness will not have to be suppressed. We must change the nature of mankind so that it is not naturally selfish. Together we must come up with a better way of raising our children.

As usual, I apologize in advance when my opinions may be perceived as offensive. I am about to express some of my opinions on raising children and they may differ from yours.

I do not declare my way better than anyone else's. Together we must find better ways, and to do this we must express our opinions and listen to the opinions of others. I am not a child psychologist, and even they don't have all the answers. If we want peace for the future, the way we raise our children will have to be addressed, because they are the future. To maximize the potential of the future we must learn from the past.

Let's look back in time for a moment and examine one method of raising children. "Spare the rod; spoil the child" is the way I've always heard the expression that summed up a commonly accepted philosophy toward raising children. This method resulted in people with terrible dispositions who make very selfish choices, as we witness in today's society. This method of beating a helpless person into submission perpetuates the control the few have upon the many by embedding a fear of authority, just or unjust. If a parent is wrong and punishes a child enough times for doing right or what is natural, wouldn't a very young child accept wrong as right or change his nature to avoid punishment? The same wrong is accepted in our adult society. Our government abuses and neglects us, but we are too scared to speak up or act on our rights as Americans and force it to provide for our safety and happiness. It is time to re-examine our customs.

To illustrate how we can reexamine accepted methods that produce undesirable results, we will go to the Bible to read more into this "spare the rod" issue. I am not advocating the Bible as an authority on the subject, nor am I condemning the contents of this book that means so much to so many. But, I believe it has been instrumental in perpetuating this mentality. Proverbs 13:24-25 in the New International Version reads, "He who spares the rod hates his son (24), but he who loves him is careful to discipline him (25)." Solomon, who is considered to have been wise, is given credit for these words. But somehow the wisdom was lost or manipulated as the concept was passed down through time.

As I did not know it, many may not know the second part of this saying. Also, the first part is different from the way I heard it. Maybe there is another verse that reads the way I heard it, but for now these two verses will do. In reading these verses as written, we realize the words *love* and *careful* are the most important words included with the word *discipline*. The word *rod* in my Bible is explained as training by word or deed. So, in loving your child or the child that you are helping raise, you will be careful not to disturb the initial peaceful disposition that this person possessed from birth. It never said to beat your children into submission to make them better people. And it surely didn't mean to criminally abuse them, because that will do wonders for their psychological development. There must be a better way to raise children.

Remember the situation I was in the day my peace came? Even though I was subjected to some of the "spare the rod" upbringing, I chose not to abuse my child in that way. Because I was also introduced to better ways of raising children, I am empowered to make better choices. Let me explain one of the ways that I think is better. When I was in third grade, my teacher was faced with yet another young person who could not control his energy and imagination—me. One day I brought a handmade martial arts weapon to school and someone told on me. She asked me for the two broomstick pieces with a chain nailed into the ends, and I produced them from the crotch of my pants. She confiscated them and sentenced me to writing my multiplication tables so many times that I can't remember the number of times. But I learned not to bring weapons to school and to multiply well. This teacher was never given the status of Solomon, but that day she was very wise. She was able to teach without useless punishment. She taught me a better way.

The system of punishment and reward is one of the many customs that will have to be rehabilitated in our effort to create a peaceful society. Children and adults can also learn by example. If the example they are learning from is selfish, selfishness is learned. Every generation of human beings must battle its selfishness so that the next generation will have less of this enemy to fight. This process must continue until the very nature of man has been changed. Then there will be everlasting peace.

In writing this book, I may have backed myself into the corner of having to design peace for the nation and the World. The absence of peace has reduced it to being just a notion defined as the end of a war. So to satisfy this requirement that war ends in peace, I end this New

Revolutionary War that I have declared on selfishness, separation, and ignorance with peace. But as you can see, peace means so much more to me. It is a source of strength and is the medium that should surround us when we unite.

The Idea of uniting as a corporate democracy to combat capitalistic selfishness is a major battle in the war. But it is the easiest one. Fighting this easy battle first, or simultaneously with the battles we must fight within ourselves to suppress our selfishness, will give us the courage and confidence we need to succeed in the war.

When The Idea was explained, the definition of capitalism was included. Examining the definition at that time was too distracting from The Idea that you waited so patiently for. But here at the end of my desperate attempt to unite the people, I will dissect it for incentive purposes.

Capitalism is defined as an economic system characterized by private or corporate ownership of capital goods, by investments that are determined by private decision, and by prices, production, and the distribution of goods that are determined mainly by competition in a free market. From this definition we learn:

If we don't own the capital goods ...

If we're not one of the private individuals making significant investment decisions ...

If we don't control the competition in the free market that controls the prices, production, and distribution of goods and/or services ...

We are just victims of this economic system.

Most of the people in the United States of America and the World are victims of capitalism and the few that it benefits. This system limits or excludes the contributions that billions of people could make to our community by making it so hard for them to supply their needs and wants and those of their families. It encourages everyone to victimize each other to become one of the few. If we unite peacefully we can stop this victimization.

Thank you for your patience and hopefully for your understanding of The Idea. In conclusion, until we unite, our enemies—selfishness, separation, ignorance, and human nature—will continue their reign of terror on our society, our economics, and our ability to govern ourselves as a democracy. We can unite, save our community, and protect our future! I hope that this book encourages everyone to peek out of his or her doorway. Once we see how many other people are considering stepping out to defeat our common enemies, we will be encouraged to sign a Declaration of Dependence and fight this New Revolutionary War.

AFTERWORD

My website address is: http://www.johngcurry.us.

Appendix I

The U.S. National Archives & Records Administration provides transcriptions of this and other documents in their original form. Some words may be misspelled or obsolete. 'Notes' have also been provided for clarity. The author has only made an honest effort to provide the readers with a reliable copy of this document that belongs to all Americans.

The Declaration of Independence

IN CONGRESS, July 4, 1776.

The unanimous Declaration of the thirteen united States of America,

When in the Course of human events, it becomes necessary for one people to dissolve the political bands which have connected them with another, and to assume among the powers of the earth, the separate and equal station to which the Laws of Nature and of Nature's God entitle them, a decent respect to the opinions of mankind requires that they should declare the causes which impel them to the separation.

We hold these truths to be self-evident, that all men are created equal, that they are endowed by their Creator with certain unalienable Rights, that among these are Life, Liberty and the pursuit of Happiness.—That to secure these rights, Governments are instituted among Men, deriving their just powers from the consent of the governed, —That whenever any Form of Government becomes destructive of these ends, it is the Right of the People to alter or to abolish it, and to institute new Government, laying its foundation on such principles and organizing its powers in such form, as to them shall seem most likely to effect their Safety and Happiness. Prudence, indeed, will dictate that Governments long established should not be changed for light and transient causes; and accordingly all experience hath shewn, that mankind are more disposed to suffer, while evils are sufferable, than to right themselves by abolishing the forms to which they are accustomed. But when a long train of abuses and usurpations, pursuing invariably the same Object evinces a design to reduce them under absolute Despotism, it is their right, it is their duty, to throw off such Government, and to provide new Guards for their future security.—Such has been the patient sufferance of these Colonies; and such is now the necessity which constrains them to alter their former Systems of Government. The history of the present King of Great Britain is a history of repeated injuries and usurpations, all having in direct object the establishment of an absolute Tyranny over these States. To prove this, let Facts be submitted to a candid world.

He has refused his Assent to Laws, the most whole-some and necessary for the public good.

He has forbidden his Governors to pass Laws of imme-diate and pressing importance, unless suspended in their operation till his Assent should be obtained; and when so suspended, he has utterly neglected to attend to them.

He has refused to pass other Laws for the accommodation of large districts of people, unless those people would relinquish the right of Representation in the Legislature, a right inestimable to them and formidable to tyrants only.

He has called together legislative bodies at places unusual, uncomfortable, and distant from the depository of their public Records, for the sole purpose of fatiguing them into compliance with his measures.

He has dissolved Representative Houses repeatedly, for opposing with manly firmness his invasions on the rights of the people.

He has refused for a long time, after such dissolutions, to cause others to be elected; whereby the Legislative powers, incapable of Annihilation, have returned to the People at large for their exercise; the State remaining in the mean time exposed to all the dangers of invasion from without, and convulsions within.

He has endeavoured to prevent the population of these States; for that purpose obstructing the Laws for Naturalization of Foreigners; refusing to pass others to encourage their migrations hither, and raising the conditions of new Appropriations of Lands.

He has obstructed the Administration of Justice, by refusing his Assent to Laws for establishing Judiciary powers.

He has made Judges dependent on his Will alone, for the tenure of their offices, and the amount and payment of their salaries.

He has erected a multitude of New Offices, and sent hither swarms of Officers to harrass our people, and eat out their substance.

He has kept among us, in times of peace, Standing Armies without the Consent of our legislatures.

He has affected to render the Military independent of and superior to the Civil power.

He has combined with others to subject us to a jurisdiction foreign to our constitution, and unacknowledged by our laws; giving his Assent to their Acts of pretended Legislation:

For Quartering large bodies of armed troops among us:

For protecting them, by a mock Trial, from punishment for any Murders which they should commit on the Inhabitants of these States:

For cutting off our Trade with all parts of the world:

For imposing Taxes on us without our Consent:

For depriving us in many cases, of the benefits of Trial by Jury:

For transporting us beyond Seas to be tried for pretended offences

For abolishing the free System of English Laws in a neighbouring Province, establishing therein an Arbitrary government, and enlarging its Boundaries so as to render it at once an example and fit instrument for introducing the same absolute rule into these Colonies:

For taking away our Charters, abolishing our most valuable Laws, and altering fundamentally the Forms of our Governments:

For suspending our own Legislatures, and declaring themselves invested with power to legislate for us in all cases whatsoever.

He has abdicated Government here, by declaring us out of his Protection and waging War against us.

He has plundered our seas, ravaged our Coasts, burnt our towns, and destroyed the lives of our people.

He is at this time transporting large Armies of foreign Mercenaries to compleat the works of death, desolation and tyranny, already begun with circumstances of Cruelty

& perfidy scarcely paralleled in the most barbarous ages, and totally unworthy the Head of a civilized nation.

He has constrained our fellow Citizens taken Captive on the high Seas to bear Arms against their Country, to become the executioners of their friends and Brethren, or to fall themselves by their Hands.

He has excited domestic insurrections amongst us, and has endeavoured to bring on the inhabitants of our frontiers, the merciless Indian Savages, whose known rule of warfare, is an undistinguished destruction of all ages, sexes and conditions.

In every stage of these Oppressions We have Petitioned for Redress in the most humble terms: Our repeated Petitions have been answered only by repeated injury. A Prince whose character is thus marked by every act which may define a Tyrant, is unfit to be the ruler of a free people.

Nor have We been wanting in attentions to our Brittish brethren. We have warned them from time to time of attempts by their legislature to extend an unwarrantable jurisdiction over us. We have reminded them of the circumstances of our emigration and settlement here. We have appealed to their native justice and magnanimity, and we have conjured them by the ties of our common kindred to disavow these usurpations, which, would inevitably interrupt our connections and correspondence. They too have been deaf to the voice of justice and of consanguinity. We must, therefore, acquiesce in the necessity, which denounces our Separation, and hold them, as we hold the rest of mankind, Enemies in War, in Peace Friends.

We, therefore, the Representatives of the united States of America, in General Congress, Assembled, appealing to the Supreme Judge of the world for the rectitude of our intentions, do, in the Name, and by Authority of the good People of these Colonies, solemnly publish and declare, That these United Colonies are, and of Right ought to be

Free and Independent States; that they are Absolved from all Allegiance to the British Crown, and that all political connection between them and the State of Great Britain, is and ought to be totally dissolved; and that as Free and Independent States, they have full Power to levy War, conclude Peace, contract Alliances, establish Commerce, and to do all other Acts and Things which Independent States may of right do. And for the support of this Declaration, with a firm reliance on the protection of divine Providence, we mutually pledge to each other our Lives, our Fortunes and our sacred Honor.

There are 56 signatures:

Column 1

(Georgia)
Button Gwinnett
Lyman Hall
George Walton

Column 2

(North Carolina)
William Hooper
Joseph Hewes
John Penn

(South Carolina)
Edward Rutledge
Thomas Heyward, Jr.
Thomas Lynch, Jr.
Arthur Middleton

Column 3

(Massachusetts)
John Hancock

(Maryland)
Samuel Chase
William Paca
Thomas Stone
Charles Carroll of Carrollton

(Virginia)
George Wythe
Richard Henry Lee
Thomas Jefferson
Benjamin Harrison
Thomas Nelson, Jr.
Francis Lightfoot Lee
Carter Braxton

Column 4

(Pennsylvania)
Robert Morris
Benjamin Rush
Benjamin Franklin
John Morton
George Clymer
James Smith
George Taylor
James Wilson
George Ross

(Delaware)
Caesar Rodney

George Read
Thomas McKean

Column 5

(New York)
William Floyd
Philip Livingston
Francis Lewis
Lewis Morris

(New Jersey)
Richard Stockton
John Witherspoon
Francis Hopkinson
John Hart
Abraham Clark

Column 6

(New Hampshire)
Josiah Bartlett
William Whipple

(Massachusetts)
Samuel Adams
John Adams
Robert Treat Paine
Elbridge Gerry

(Rhode Island)
Stephen Hopkins
William Ellery

(Connecticut)
Roger Sherman
Samuel Huntington
William Williams
Oliver Wolcott

(New Hampshire)
Matthew Thornton

APPENDIX II

The U.S. National Archives & Records Administration provides transcriptions of this and other documents in their original form. Some words may be misspelled or obsolete. 'Notes' have also been provided for clarity. The author has only made an honest effort to provide the readers with a reliable copy of this document that belongs to all Americans.

The Constitution of the United States

We the People of the United States, in Order to form a more perfect Union, establish Justice, insure domestic Tranquility, provide for the common defense, promote the general Welfare, and secure the Blessings of Liberty to ourselves and our Posterity, do ordain and establish this Constitution for the United States of America.

Article. I.

Section. 1.

All legislative Powers herein granted shall be vested in a Congress of the United States, which shall consist of a Senate and House of Representatives.

Section. 2.

The House of Representatives shall be composed of Members chosen every second Year by the People of the several States, and the Electors in each State shall have the Qualifications requisite for Electors of the most numerous Branch of the State Legislature.

No Person shall be a Representative who shall not have attained to the Age of twenty five Years, and been seven Years a Citizen of the United States, and who shall not, when elected, be an Inhabitant of that State in which he shall be chosen.

Representatives and direct Taxes shall be apportioned among the several States which may be included within this Union, according to their respective Numbers, which shall be determined by adding to the whole Number of free Persons, including those bound to Service for a Term of Years, and excluding Indians not taxed, three fifths of all other Persons. The actual Enumeration shall be made within three Years after the first Meeting of the Congress of the United States, and within every subsequent Term of ten Years, in such Manner as they shall by Law direct. The Number of Representatives shall not exceed one for every thirty Thousand, but each State shall have at Least one Representative; and until such enumeration shall be made, the State of New Hampshire shall be entitled to chuse three, Massachusetts eight, Rhode-Island and Providence Plantations one, Connecticut five, New-York six, New Jersey four, Pennsylvania eight, Delaware one, Maryland six, Virginia ten, North Carolina five, South Carolina five, and Georgia three.

When vacancies happen in the Representation from any State, the Executive Authority thereof shall issue Writs of Election to fill such Vacancies.

The House of Representatives shall chuse their Speaker and other Officers; and shall have the sole Power of Impeachment.

Section. 3.

The Senate of the United States shall be composed of two Senators from each State, chosen by the Legislature thereof for six Years; and each Senator shall have one Vote.

Immediately after they shall be assembled in Consequence of the first Election, they shall be divided as equally as may be into three Classes. The Seats of the Senators of the first Class shall be vacated at the Expiration of the second Year, of the second Class at the Expiration of the fourth Year, and of the third Class at the Expiration of the sixth Year, so that one third may be chosen every second Year; and if Vacancies happen by Resignation, or otherwise, during the Recess of the Legislature of any State, the Executive thereof may make temporary Appointments until the next Meeting of the Legislature, which shall then fill such Vacancies.

No Person shall be a Senator who shall not have attained to the Age of thirty Years, and been nine Years a Citizen of the United States, and who shall not, when elected, be an Inhabitant of that State for which he shall be chosen.

The Vice President of the United States shall be President of the Senate, but shall have no Vote, unless they be equally divided.

The Senate shall chuse their other Officers, and also a President pro tempore, in the Absence of the Vice President, or when he shall exercise the Office of President of the United States.

The Senate shall have the sole Power to try all Impeachments. When sitting for that Purpose, they shall be on Oath or Affirmation. When the President of the United States is tried, the Chief Justice shall preside: And no Person shall be convicted without the Concurrence of two thirds of the Members present.

Judgment in Cases of Impeachment shall not extend further than to removal from Office, and disqualification to hold and enjoy any Office of honor, Trust or Profit under the United States: but the Party convicted shall nevertheless be liable and subject to Indictment, Trial, Judgment and Punishment, according to Law.

Section. 4.

The Times, Places and Manner of holding Elections for Senators and Representatives, shall be prescribed in each State by the Legislature thereof; but the Congress may at any time by Law make or alter such Regulations, except as to the Places of chusing Senators.

The Congress shall assemble at least once in every Year, and such Meeting shall be on the first Monday in December, unless they shall by Law appoint a different Day.

Section. 5.

Each House shall be the Judge of the Elections, Returns and Qualifications of its own Members, and a Majority of each shall constitute a Quorum to do Business; but a smaller Number may adjourn from day to day, and may be authorized to compel the Attendance of absent Members, in such Manner, and under such Penalties as each House may provide.

Each House may determine the Rules of its Proceedings, punish its Members for disorderly Behaviour, and, with the Concurrence of two thirds, expel a Member.

Each House shall keep a Journal of its Proceedings, and from time to time publish the same, excepting such Parts as may in their Judgment require Secrecy; and the Yeas and Nays of the Members of either House on any question shall, at the Desire of one fifth of those Present, be entered on the Journal.

Neither House, during the Session of Congress, shall, without the Consent of the other, adjourn for more than three days, nor to any other Place than that in which the two Houses shall be sitting.

Section. 6.

The Senators and Representatives shall receive a Compensation for their Services, to be ascertained by Law, and paid out of the Treasury of the United States. They shall in all Cases, except Treason, Felony and Breach of the Peace, be privileged from Arrest during their Attendance at the Session of their respective Houses, and in going to and returning from the same; and for any Speech or Debate in either House, they shall not be questioned in any other Place.

No Senator or Representative shall, during the Time
for which he was elected, be appointed to any civil Office
under the Authority of the United States, which shall have
been created, or the Emoluments whereof shall have been
encreased during such time; and no Person holding any
Office under the United States, shall be a Member of either
House during his Continuance in Office.

Section. 7.

All Bills for raising Revenue shall originate in the
House of Representatives; but the Senate may propose or
concur with Amendments as on other Bills.

Every Bill which shall have passed the House of
Representatives and the Senate, shall, before it become a
Law, be presented to the President of the United States:
If he approve he shall sign it, but if not he shall return it,
with his Objections to that House in which it shall have
originated, who shall enter the Objections at large on
their Journal, and proceed to reconsider it.If after such
Reconsideration two thirds of that House shall agree to
pass the Bill, it shall be sent, together with the Objections,
to the other House, by which it shall likewise be reconsid-
ered, and if approved by two thirds of that House, it shall
become a Law. But in all such Cases the Votes of both
Houses shall be determined by yeas and Nays, and the
Names of the Persons voting for and against the Bill shall
be entered on the Journal of each House respectively. If
any Bill shall not be returned by the President within ten
Days (Sundays excepted) after it shall have been presented
to him, the Same shall be a Law, in like Manner as if he
had signed it, unless the Congress by their Adjournment
prevent its Return, in which Case it shall not be a Law.

Every Order, Resolution, or Vote to which the Concurrence of the Senate and House of Representatives may be necessary (except on a question of Adjournment) shall be presented to the President of the United States; and before the Same shall take Effect, shall be approved by him, or being disapproved by him, shall be repassed by two thirds of the Senate and House of Representatives, according to the Rules and Limitations prescribed in the Case of a Bill.

Section. 8.

The Congress shall have Power To lay and collect Taxes, Duties, Imposts and Excises, to pay the Debts and provide for the common Defence and general Welfare of the United States; but all Duties, Imposts and Excises shall be uniform throughout the United States;

To borrow Money on the credit of the United States;

To regulate Commerce with foreign Nations, and among the several States, and with the Indian Tribes;

To establish an uniform Rule of Naturalization, and uniform Laws on the subject of Bankruptcies throughout the United States;

To coin Money, regulate the Value thereof, and of foreign Coin, and fix the Standard of Weights and Measures;

To provide for the Punishment of counterfeiting the Securities and current Coin of the United States;

To establish Post Offices and post Roads;

To promote the Progress of Science and useful Arts, by securing for limited Times to Authors and Inventors the exclusive Right to their respective Writings and Discoveries;

To constitute Tribunals inferior to the supreme Court;

To define and punish Piracies and Felonies committed on the high Seas, and Offences against the Law of Nations;

To declare War, grant Letters of Marque and Reprisal, and make Rules concerning Captures on Land and Water;

To raise and support Armies, but no Appropriation of Money to that Use shall be for a longer Term than two Years;

To provide and maintain a Navy;

To make Rules for the Government and Regulation of the land and naval Forces;

To provide for calling forth the Militia to execute the Laws of the Union, suppress Insurrections and repel Invasions;

To provide for organizing, arming, and disciplining, the Militia, and for governing such Part of them as may be employed in the Service of the United States, reserving to the States respectively, the Appointment of the Officers, and the Authority of training the Militia according to the discipline prescribed by Congress;

To exercise exclusive Legislation in all Cases whatso-ever, over such District (not exceeding ten Miles square) as may, by Cession of particular States, and the Acceptance of Congress, become the Seat of the Government of the

United States, and to exercise like Authority over all Places purchased by the Consent of the Legislature of the State in which the Same shall be, for the Erection of Forts, Magazines, Arsenals, dock-Yards, and other needful Buildings;—And

To make all Laws which shall be necessary and proper for carrying into Execution the foregoing Powers, and all other Powers vested by this Constitution in the Government of the United States, or in any Department or Officer thereof.

Section. 9.

The Migration or Importation of such Persons as any of the States now existing shall think proper to admit, shall not be prohibited by the Congress prior to the Year one thousand eight hundred and eight, but a Tax or duty may be imposed on such Importation, not exceeding ten dollars for each Person.

The Privilege of the Writ of Habeas Corpus shall not be suspended, unless when in Cases of Rebellion or Invasion the public Safety may require it.

No Bill of Attainder or ex post facto Law shall be passed.

No Capitation, or other direct, Tax shall be laid, unless in Proportion to the Census or enumeration herein before directed to be taken.

No Tax or Duty shall be laid on Articles exported from any State.

No Preference shall be given by any Regulation of Commerce or Revenue to the Ports of one State over those of another; nor shall Vessels bound to, or from, one State, be obliged to enter, clear, or pay Duties in another.

No Money shall be drawn from the Treasury, but in Consequence of Appropriations made by Law; and a regular Statement and Account of the Receipts and Expenditures of all public Money shall be published from time to time.

No Title of Nobility shall be granted by the United States: And no Person holding any Office of Profit or Trust under them, shall, without the Consent of the Congress, accept of any present, Emolument, Office, or Title, of any kind whatever, from any King, Prince, or foreign State.

Section. 10.

No State shall enter into any Treaty, Alliance, or Confederation; grant Letters of Marque and Reprisal; coin Money; emit Bills of Credit; make any Thing but gold and silver Coin a Tender in Payment of Debts; pass any Bill of Attainder, ex post facto Law, or Law impairing the Obligation of Contracts, or grant any Title of Nobility.

No State shall, without the Consent of the Congress, lay any Imposts or Duties on Imports or Exports, except what may be absolutely necessary for executing it's inspection Laws: and the net Produce of all Duties and Imposts, laid by any State on Imports or Exports, shall be for the Use of the Treasury of the United States; and all such Laws shall be subject to the Revision and Controul of the Congress.

No State shall, without the Consent of Congress, lay any Duty of Tonnage, keep Troops, or Ships of War in time of Peace, enter into any Agreement or Compact with another State, or with a foreign Power, or engage in War, unless actually invaded, or in such imminent Danger as will not admit of delay.

Article. II.

Section. 1.

The executive Power shall be vested in a President of the United States of America. He shall hold his Office during the Term of four Years, and, together with the Vice President, chosen for the same Term, be elected, as follows:

Each State shall appoint, in such Manner as the Legislature thereof may direct, a Number of Electors, equal to the whole Number of Senators and Representatives to which the State may be entitled in the Congress: but no Senator or Representative, or Person holding an Office of Trust or Profit under the United States, shall be appointed an Elector.

The Electors shall meet in their respective States, and vote by Ballot for two Persons, of whom one at least shall not be an Inhabitant of the same State with themselves. And they shall make a List of all the Persons voted for, and of the Number of Votes for each; which List they shall sign and certify, and transmit sealed to the Seat of the Government of the United States, directed to the President of the Senate. The President of the Senate shall, in the Presence of the Senate and House of Representatives, open all the Certificates, and the Votes shall then be counted. The Person having the greatest Number of Votes shall be the President, if such Number be a Majority of the whole Number of Electors appointed; and if there be more than one who have such Majority, and have an equal Number of Votes, then the House of Representatives shall immediately chuse by Ballot one of them for President; and if no Person have a Majority, then from the five highest on the List the said House shall in like Manner chuse the President. But in chusing the President, the Votes shall be taken by States, the Representation from each State having one Vote; A quorum for this purpose shall consist of a Member or Members from two thirds of the States, and a Majority of all the States shall be necessary to a Choice. In every Case, after the Choice of the President, the Person having the greatest Number of Votes of the Electors shall be the Vice President. But if there should remain two or more who have equal Votes, the Senate shall chuse from them by Ballot the Vice President.

The Congress may determine the Time of chusing the Electors, and the Day on which they shall give their Votes; which Day shall be the same throughout the United States.

No Person except a natural born Citizen, or a Citizen of the United States, at the time of the Adoption of this Constitution, shall be eligible to the Office of President; neither shall any Person be eligible to that Office who shall not have attained to the Age of thirty five Years, and been fourteen Years a Resident within the United States.

In Case of the Removal of the President from Office, or of his Death, Resignation, or Inability to discharge the Powers and Duties of the said Office, the Same shall devolve on the Vice President, and the Congress may by Law provide for the Case of Removal, Death, Resignation or Inability, both of the President and Vice President, declaring what Officer shall then act as President, and such Officer shall act accordingly, until the Disability be removed, or a President shall be elected.

The President shall, at stated Times, receive for his Services, a Compensation, which shall neither be increased nor diminished during the Period for which he shall have been elected, and he shall not receive within that Period any other Emolument from the United States, or any of them.

Before he enter on the Execution of his Office, he shall take the following Oath or Affirmation:—"I do solemnly swear (or affirm) that I will faithfully execute the Office of President of the United States, and will to the best of my Ability, preserve, protect and defend the Constitution of the United States."

Section. 2.

The President shall be Commander in Chief of the Army and Navy of the United States, and of the Militia of the several States, when called into the actual Service of the United States; he may require the Opinion, in writing, of the principal Officer in each of the executive Departments, upon any Subject relating to the Duties of their respective Offices, and he shall have Power to grant Reprieves and Pardons for Offences against the United States, except in Cases of Impeachment.

He shall have Power, by and with the Advice and Consent of the Senate, to make Treaties, provided two thirds of the Senators present concur; and he shall nominate, and by and with the Advice and Consent of the Senate, shall appoint Ambassadors, other public Ministers and Consuls, Judges of the supreme Court, and all other Officers of the United States, whose Appointments are not herein otherwise provided for, and which shall be established by Law: but the Congress may by Law vest the Appointment of such inferior Officers, as they think proper, in the President alone, in the Courts of Law, or in the Heads of Departments.

The President shall have Power to fill up all Vacancies that may happen during the Recess of the Senate, by granting Commissions which shall expire at the End of their next Session.

Section. 3.

He shall from time to time give to the Congress Information of the State of the Union, and recommend to their Consideration such Measures as he shall judge necessary and expedient; he may, on extraordinary Occasions, convene both Houses, or either of them, and in Case of Disagreement between them, with Respect to the Time of Adjournment, he may adjourn them to such Time as he shall think proper; he shall receive Ambassadors and other public Ministers; he shall take Care that the Laws be faithfully executed, and shall Commission all the Officers of the United States.

Section. 4.

The President, Vice President and all civil Officers of the United States, shall be removed from Office on Impeachment for, and Conviction of, Treason, Bribery, or other high Crimes and Misdemeanors.

Article III.

Section. 1.

The judicial Power of the United States shall be vested in one supreme Court, and in such inferior Courts as the Congress may from time to time ordain and establish. The Judges, both of the supreme and inferior Courts, shall hold their Offices during good Behaviour, and shall, at stated

Times, receive for their Services a Compensation, which shall not be diminished during their Continuance in Office.

Section. 2.

The judicial Power shall extend to all Cases, in Law and Equity, arising under this Constitution, the Laws of the United States, and Treaties made, or which shall be made, under their Authority;—to all Cases affecting Ambassadors, other public Ministers and Consuls;—to all Cases of admiralty and maritime Jurisdiction;—to Controversies to which the United States shall be a Party;—to Controversies between two or more States;—between a State and Citizens of another State;—between Citizens of different States;—between Citizens of the same State claiming Lands under Grants of different States, and between a State, or the Citizens thereof, and foreign States, Citizens or Subjects.

In all Cases affecting Ambassadors, other public Ministers and Consuls, and those in which a State shall be Party, the supreme Court shall have original Jurisdiction. In all the other Cases before mentioned, the supreme Court shall have appellate Jurisdiction, both as to Law and Fact, with such Exceptions, and under such Regulations as the Congress shall make.

The Trial of all Crimes, except in Cases of Impeachment, shall be by Jury; and such Trial shall be held in the State where the said Crimes shall have been committed; but when not committed within any State, the Trial shall be at such Place or Places as the Congress may by Law have directed.

Section. 3.

Treason against the United States, shall consist only in levying War against them, or in adhering to their Enemies, giving them Aid and Comfort. No Person shall be convicted of Treason unless on the Testimony of two Witnesses to the same overt Act, or on Confession in open Court.

The Congress shall have Power to declare the Punishment of Treason, but no Attainder of Treason shall work Corruption of Blood, or Forfeiture except during the Life of the Person attainted.

Article. IV.

Section. 1.
Full Faith and Credit shall be given in each State to the public Acts, Records, and judicial Proceedings of every other State. And the Congress may by general Laws prescribe the Manner in which such Acts, Records and Proceedings shall be proved, and the Effect thereof.

Section. 2.
The Citizens of each State shall be entitled to all Privileges and Immunities of Citizens in the several States.

A Person charged in any State with Treason, Felony, or other Crime, who shall flee from Justice, and be found in another State, shall on Demand of the executive Authority of the State from which he fled, be delivered up, to be removed to the State having Jurisdiction of the Crime.

No Person held to Service or Labour in one State, under the Laws thereof, escaping into another, shall, in Consequence of any Law or Regulation therein, be discharged from such Service or Labour, but shall be delivered up on Claim of the Party to whom such Service or Labour may be due.

Section. 3.

New States may be admitted by the Congress into this Union; but no new State shall be formed or erected within the Jurisdiction of any other State; nor any State be formed by the Junction of two or more States, or Parts of States, without the Consent of the Legislatures of the States concerned as well as of the Congress.

The Congress shall have Power to dispose of and make all needful Rules and Regulations respecting the Territory or other Property belonging to the United States; and nothing in this Constitution shall be so construed as to Prejudice any Claims of the United States, or of any particular State.

Section. 4.

The United States shall guarantee to every State in this Union a Republican Form of Government, and shall protect each of them against Invasion; and on Application of the Legislature, or of the Executive (when the Legislature cannot be convened), against domestic Violence.

Article. V.

The Congress, whenever two thirds of both Houses shall deem it necessary, shall propose Amendments to this Constitution, or, on the Application of the Legislatures of two thirds of the several States, shall call a Convention for proposing Amendments, which, in either Case, shall be valid to all Intents and Purposes, as Part of this Constitution, when ratified by the Legislatures of three fourths of the several States, or by Conventions in three fourths thereof, as the one or the other Mode of Ratification may be proposed by the Congress; Provided that no Amendment which may be made prior to the Year One thousand eight hundred and eight shall in any Manner affect the first and fourth Clauses in the Ninth Section of the first Article; and that no State, without its Consent, shall be deprived of its equal Suffrage in the Senate.

Article. VI.

All Debts contracted and Engagements entered into, before the Adoption of this Constitution, shall be as valid against the United States under this Constitution, as under the Confederation.

This Constitution, and the Laws of the United States which shall be made in Pursuance thereof; and all Treaties made, or which shall be made, under the Authority of the United States, shall be the supreme Law of the Land; and the Judges in every State shall be bound thereby, any Thing in the Constitution or Laws of any State to the Contrary notwithstanding.

The Senators and Representatives before mentioned, and the Members of the several State Legislatures, and all executive and judicial Officers, both of the United States and of the several States, shall be bound by Oath or Affirmation, to support this Constitution; but no religious Test shall ever be required as a Qualification to any Office or public Trust under the United States.

Article. VII.

The Ratification of the Conventions of nine States, shall be sufficient for the Establishment of this Constitution between the States so ratifying the Same.

The Word, "the," being interlined between the seventh and eighth Lines of the first Page, the Word "Thirty" being partly written on an Erazure in the fifteenth Line of the first Page, The Words "is tried" being interlined between the thirty second and thirty third Lines of the first Page and the Word "the" being interlined between the forty third and forty fourth Lines of the second Page.

Attest William Jackson Secretary

Done in Convention by the Unanimous Consent of the States present the Seventeenth Day of September in the Year of our Lord one thousand seven hundred and Eighty seven and of the Independence of the United States of America the Twelfth In witness whereof We have hereunto subscribed our Names,

(The signers)

George Washington
President and deputy from Virginia

(Delaware)
Geo. Read
Gunning Bedford Jun
John Dickinson
Richard Bassett
Jaco. Broom

(Maryland)
James McHenry
Dan. of St Thos. Jenifer
Danl. Carroll

(Virginia)
John Blair
James Madison Jr.

(North Carolina)
Wm. Blount
Richd Dobbs Spaight
Hu. Williamson

(South Carolina)
J. Rutledge
Charles Cotesworth Pinckney
Charles Pinckney
Pierce Butler

(Georgia)
William Few
Abr Baldwin

(New Hampshire)
John Langdon
Nicholas Gilman

(Massachusetts)
Nathaniel Gorham
Rufus King

(Connecticut)
Wm. Saml. Johnson
Roger Sherman

(New York)
Alexander Hamilton

(New Jersey)
Wil: Livingston
David Brearley
Wm. Paterson
Jona. Dayton

(Pennsylvania)
B. Franklin
Thomas Mifflin
Robt. Morris
Geo. Clymer
Thos. FitzSimons
Jared Ingersoll
James Wilson
Gouv. Morris

The first ten amendments to the Constitution are known as The Bill of Rights, ratified December 15, 1791.

Amendment I

Congress shall make no law respecting an establishment of religion, or prohibiting the free exercise thereof; or abridging the freedom of speech, or of the press; or the right of the people peaceably to assemble, and to petition the Government for a redress of grievances.

Amendment II

A well regulated Militia, being necessary to the security of a free State, the right of the people to keep and bear Arms, shall not be infringed.

Amendment III

No Soldier shall, in time of peace be quartered in any house, without the consent of the Owner, nor in time of war, but in a manner to be prescribed by law.

Amendment IV

The right of the people to be secure in their persons, houses, papers, and effects, against unreasonable searches and seizures, shall not be violated, and no Warrants shall issue, but upon probable cause, supported by Oath or affirmation, and particularly describing the place to be searched, and the persons or things to be seized.

Amendment V

No person shall be held to answer for a capital, or otherwise infamous crime, unless on a presentment or indictment of a Grand Jury, except in cases arising in the land or naval forces, or in the Militia, when in actual service in time of War or public danger; nor shall any person be subject for the same offence to be twice put in jeopardy of life or limb; nor shall be compelled in any criminal case to be a witness against himself, nor be deprived of life, liberty, or property, without due process of law; nor shall private property be taken for public use, without just compensation.

Amendment VI

In all criminal prosecutions, the accused shall enjoy the right to a speedy and public trial, by an impartial jury of the State and district wherein the crime shall have been committed, which district shall have been previously ascertained by law, and to be informed of the nature and cause of the accusation; to be confronted with the witnesses against him; to have compulsory process for obtaining witnesses in his favor, and to have the Assistance of Counsel for his defence.

Amendment VII

In Suits at common law, where the value in controversy shall exceed twenty dollars, the right of trial by jury shall be preserved, and no fact tried by a jury, shall be otherwise re-examined in any Court of the United States, than according to the rules of the common law.

Amendment VIII

Excessive bail shall not be required, nor excessive fines imposed, nor cruel and unusual punishments inflicted.

Amendment IX

The enumeration in the Constitution, of certain rights, shall not be construed to deny or disparage others retained by the people.

Amendment X

The powers not delegated to the United States by the Constitution, nor prohibited by it to the States, are reserved to the States respectively, or to the people.

Amendment XI

Passed by Congress March 4, 1794. Ratified February 7, 1795.

Note: Article III, section 2, of the Constitution was modified by amendment 11.

The Judicial power of the United States shall not be construed to extend to any suit in law or equity, commenced or prosecuted against one of the United States by Citizens of another State, or by Citizens or Subjects of any Foreign State.

Amendment XII

Passed by Congress December 9, 1803. Ratified June 15, 1804.

Note: A portion of Article II, section 1 of the Constitution was superseded by the 12th amendment.

The Electors shall meet in their respective states and vote by ballot for President and Vice-President, one of whom, at least, shall not be an inhabitant of the same state with themselves; they shall name in their ballots the person voted for as President, and in distinct ballots the person voted for as Vice-President, and they shall make distinct lists of all persons voted for as President, and of all persons voted for as Vice-President, and of the number of votes for each, which lists they shall sign and certify, and transmit sealed to the seat of the government of the United States, directed to the President of the Senate; — the President of the Senate shall, in the presence of the Senate and House of Representatives, open all the certificates and the votes shall then be counted; — The person having the greatest number of votes for President, shall be the President, if such number be a majority of the whole number of Electors appointed; and if no person have such majority, then from the persons having the highest numbers not exceeding three on the list of those voted for as President, the House of Representatives shall choose immediately, by ballot, the President. But in choosing the President, the votes shall be taken by states, the representation from each state having one vote; a quorum for this purpose shall consist of a member or members from two-thirds of the states, and a majority of all the states shall be necessary to a choice. [And if the House of Representatives shall not choose a President whenever the right of choice shall devolve upon them, before the fourth day of March next following, then the Vice-President shall act as President, as in case of the death or other constitutional disability of the President. —]* The person having the greatest number of votes as Vice-President, shall be the Vice-President, if such number be a majority of the whole number of

Electors appointed, and if no person have a majority, then from the two highest numbers on the list, the Senate shall choose the Vice-President; a quorum for the purpose shall consist of two-thirds of the whole number of Senators, and a majority of the whole number shall be necessary to a choice. But no person constitutionally ineligible to the office of President shall be eligible to that of Vice-President of the United States.

*Superseded by section 3 of the 20th amendment.

Amendment XIII

Passed by Congress January 31, 1865. Ratified December 6, 1865.

Note: A portion of Article IV, section 2, of the Constitution was superseded by the 13th amendment.

Section 1.

Neither slavery nor involuntary servitude, except as a punishment for crime whereof the party shall have been duly convicted, shall exist within the United States, or any place subject to their jurisdiction.

Section 2.

Congress shall have power to enforce this article by appropriate legislation.

Amendment XIV

Passed by Congress June 13, 1866. Ratified July 9, 1868.

Note: Article I, section 2, of the Constitution was modified by section 2 of the 14th amendment.

Section 1.

All persons born or naturalized in the United States, and subject to the jurisdiction thereof, are citizens of the United States and of the State wherein they reside. No State shall make or enforce any law which shall abridge the privileges or immunities of citizens of the United States; nor shall any State deprive any person of life, liberty, or property, without due process of law; nor deny to any person within its jurisdiction the equal protection of the laws.

Section 2.

Representatives shall be apportioned among the several States according to their respective numbers, counting the whole number of persons in each State, excluding Indians not taxed. But when the right to vote at any election for the choice of electors for President and Vice-President of the United States, Representatives in Congress, the Executive and Judicial officers of a State, or the members of the Legislature thereof, is denied to any of the male inhabitants of such State, being twenty-one years of age,* and citizens of the United States, or in any way abridged, except for participation in rebellion, or other crime, the basis of representation therein shall be reduced in the proportion which the number of such male citizens shall bear to the whole number of male citizens twenty-one years of age in such State.

Section 3.

No person shall be a Senator or Representative in Congress, or elector of President and Vice-President, or hold any office, civil or military, under the United States, or under any State, who, having previously taken an oath, as a member of Congress, or as an officer of the United States, or as a member of any State legislature, or as an executive or judicial officer of any State, to support the Constitution of the United States, shall have engaged in insurrection or rebellion against the same, or given aid or comfort to the enemies thereof. But Congress may by a vote of two-thirds of each House, remove such disability.

Section 4.

The validity of the public debt of the United States, authorized by law, including debts incurred for payment of pensions and bounties for services in suppressing insurrection or rebellion, shall not be questioned. But neither the United States nor any State shall assume or pay any debt or obligation incurred in aid of insurrection or rebellion against the United States, or any claim for the loss or emancipation of any slave; but all such debts, obligations and claims shall be held illegal and void.

Section 5.

The Congress shall have the power to enforce, by appropriate legislation, the provisions of this article.

*Changed by section 1 of the 26th amendment.

Amendment XV

Passed by Congress February 26, 1869. Ratified February 3, 1870.

Section 1.

The right of citizens of the United States to vote shall not be denied or abridged by the United States or by any State on account of race, color, or previous condition of servitude—

Section 2.

The Congress shall have the power to enforce this article by appropriate legislation.

Amendment XVI

Passed by Congress July 2, 1909. Ratified February 3, 1913.

Note: Article I, section 9, of the Constitution was modified by amendment 16.

The Congress shall have power to lay and collect taxes on incomes, from whatever source derived, without apportionment among the several States, and without regard to any census or enumeration.

Amendment XVII

Passed by Congress May 13, 1912. Ratified April 8, 1913.

Note: Article I, section 3, of the Constitution was modified by the 17th amendment.

The Senate of the United States shall be composed of two Senators from each State, elected by the people thereof, for six years; and each Senator shall have one vote. The electors in each State shall have the qualifications requisite for electors of the most numerous branch of the State legislatures.

When vacancies happen in the representation of any State in the Senate, the executive authority of such State shall issue writs of election to fill such vacancies: Provided, That the legislature of any State may empower the executive thereof to make temporary appointments until the people fill the vacancies by election as the legislature may direct.

This amendment shall not be so construed as to affect the election or term of any Senator chosen before it becomes valid as part of the Constitution.

Amendment XVIII

Passed by Congress December 18, 1917. Ratified January 16, 1919. Repealed by amendment 21.

Section 1.

After one year from the ratification of this article the manufacture, sale, or transportation of intoxicating liquors within, the importation thereof into, or the exportation thereof from the United States and all territory subject to the jurisdiction thereof for beverage purposes is hereby prohibited.

Section 2.

The Congress and the several States shall have concurrent power to enforce this article by appropriate legislation.

Section 3.

This article shall be inoperative unless it shall have been ratified as an amendment to the Constitution by the legislatures of the several States, as provided in the Constitution, within seven years from the date of the submission hereof to the States by the Congress.

Amendment XIX

Passed by Congress June 4, 1919. Ratified August 18, 1920.

The right of citizens of the United States to vote shall not be denied or abridged by the United States or by any State on account of sex.

Congress shall have power to enforce this article by appropriate legislation.

Amendment XX

Passed by Congress March 2, 1932. Ratified January 23, 1933.

Note: Article I, section 4, of the Constitution was modified by section 2 of this amendment. In addition, a portion of the 12th amendment was superseded by section 3.

Section 1.

The terms of the President and the Vice President shall end at noon on the 20th day of January, and the terms of Senators and Representatives at noon on the 3d day of January, of the years in which such terms would have ended if this article had not been ratified; and the terms of their successors shall then begin.

Section 2.

The Congress shall assemble at least once in every year, and such meeting shall begin at noon on the 3d day of January, unless they shall by law appoint a different day.

Section 3.

If, at the time fixed for the beginning of the term of the President, the President elect shall have died, the Vice President elect shall become President. If a President shall not have been chosen before the time fixed for the beginning of his term, or if the President elect shall have failed to qualify, then the Vice President elect shall act as President until a President shall have qualified; and the Congress may by law provide for the case wherein neither a President elect nor a Vice President shall have qualified, declaring who shall then act as President, or the manner in which one who is to act shall be selected, and such person shall act accordingly until a President or Vice President shall have qualified.

Section 4.

The Congress may by law provide for the case of the death of any of the persons from whom the House of Representatives may choose a President whenever the right of choice shall have devolved upon them, and for the case of the death of any of the persons from whom the Senate may choose a Vice President whenever the right of choice shall have devolved upon them.

Section 5.

Sections 1 and 2 shall take effect on the 15th day of October following the ratification of this article.

Section 6.

This article shall be inoperative unless it shall have been ratified as an amendment to the Constitution by the legislatures of three-fourths of the several States within seven years from the date of its submission.

Amendment XXI

Passed by Congress February 20, 1933. Ratified December 5, 1933.

Section 1.

The eighteenth article of amendment to the Constitution of the United States is hereby repealed.

Section 2.

The transportation or importation into any State, Territory, or Possession of the United States for delivery or use therein of intoxicating liquors, in violation of the laws thereof, is hereby prohibited.

Section 3.

This article shall be inoperative unless it shall have been ratified as an amendment to the Constitution by conventions in the several States, as provided in the Constitution, within seven years from the date of the submission hereof to the States by the Congress.

Amendment XXII

Passed by Congress March 21, 1947. Ratified February 27, 1951.

Section 1.

No person shall be elected to the office of the President more than twice, and no person who has held the office of President, or acted as President, for more than two years of a term to which some other person was elected President shall be elected to the office of President more than once. But this Article shall not apply to any person holding the office of President when this Article was proposed by Congress, and shall not prevent any person who may be holding the office of President, or acting as President, during the term within which this Article becomes operative from holding the office of President or acting as President during the remainder of such term.

Section 2.

This article shall be inoperative unless it shall have been ratified as an amendment to the Constitution by the legislatures of three-fourths of the several States within seven years from the date of its submission to the States by the Congress.

Amendment XXIII

Passed by Congress June 16, 1960. Ratified March 29, 1961.

Section 1.

The District constituting the seat of Government of the United States shall appoint in such manner as Congress may direct: A number of electors of President and Vice President equal to the whole number of Senators and Representatives in Congress to which the District would be entitled if it were a State, but in no event more than the least populous State; they shall be in addition to those appointed by the States, but they shall be considered, for the purposes of the election of President and Vice President, to be electors appointed by a State; and they shall meet in the District and perform such duties as provided by the twelfth article of amendment.

Section 2.

The Congress shall have power to enforce this article by appropriate legislation.

Amendment XXIV

Passed by Congress August 27, 1962. Ratified January 23, 1964.

Section 1.

The right of citizens of the United States to vote in any primary or other election for President or Vice President, for electors for President or Vice President, or for Senator or Representative in Congress, shall not be denied or abridged by the United States or any State by reason of failure to pay poll tax or other tax.

Section 2.

The Congress shall have power to enforce this article by appropriate legislation.

Amendment XXV

Passed by Congress July 6, 1965. Ratified February 10, 1967.

Note: Article II, section 1, of the Constitution was affected by the 25th amendment.

Section 1.

In case of the removal of the President from office or of his death or resignation, the Vice President shall become President.

Section 2.

Whenever there is a vacancy in the office of the Vice President, the President shall nominate a Vice President who shall take office upon confirmation by a majority vote of both Houses of Congress.

Section 3.

Whenever the President transmits to the President pro tempore of the Senate and the Speaker of the House of Representatives his written declaration that he is unable to discharge the powers and duties of his office, and until he transmits to them a written declaration to the contrary, such powers and duties shall be discharged by the Vice President as Acting President.

Section 4.

Whenever the Vice President and a majority of either the principal officers of the executive departments or of such other body as Congress may by law provide, transmit to the President pro tempore of the Senate and the Speaker of the House of Representatives their written declaration that the President is unable to discharge the powers and duties of his office, the Vice President shall immediately assume the powers and duties of the office as Acting President.

Thereafter, when the President transmits to the President pro tempore of the Senate and the Speaker of the House of Representatives his written declaration that no inability exists, he shall resume the powers and duties of his office unless the Vice President and a majority of either the principal officers of the executive department or of such other body as Congress may by law provide, transmit within four days to the President pro tempore of the Senate and the Speaker of the House of Representatives their written declaration that the President is unable to discharge the powers and duties of his office. Thereupon Congress shall decide the issue, assembling within forty-eight hours for that purpose if not in session. If the Congress, within twenty-one days after receipt of the latter written declaration, or, if Congress is not in session, within twenty-one days after Congress is required to assemble, determines by two-thirds vote of both Houses that the President is unable to discharge the powers and duties of his office, the Vice President shall continue to discharge the same as Acting President; otherwise, the President shall resume the powers and duties of his office.

Amendment XXVI

Passed by Congress March 23, 1971. Ratified July 1, 1971.

Note: Amendment 14, section 2, of the Constitution was modified by section 1 of the 26th amendment.

Section 1.

The right of citizens of the United States, who are eighteen years of age or older, to vote shall not be denied or abridged by the United States or by any State on account of age.

Section 2.

The Congress shall have power to enforce this article by appropriate legislation.

Amendment XXVII

Originally proposed Sept. 25, 1789. Ratified May 7, 1992.

No law, varying the compensation for the services of the Senators and Representatives, shall take effect, until an election of representatives shall have intervened.